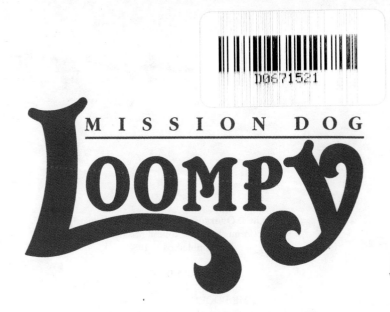

MISSION DOG
Loompy

SHEILA GROVES

AN OMF BOOK

J
F
Gro

OMF BOOKS are distributed by
OMF, 404 South Church Street, Robesonia, Pa. 19551, USA;
OMF, Belmont, The Vine, Sevenoaks, Kent, TN13 3TZ, UK;
OMF, P O Box 177, Kew East, Victoria 3102,
Australia;
and other OMF offices.

This true story is especially written for 5-8 year olds.
Published by Overseas Missionary Fellowship (IHQ) Ltd.,
2 Cluny Road, Singapore 1025, Republic of Singapore.

Printed in Singapore

Contents

CHAPTER 1

Introducing Loompy

I'm writing this from underneath Uncle Joachim's bed.

Well, it may seem funny to you, but it's where I always go when those bright flashes start up in the sky. I run as fast as ever I can, to try to get underneath before that awful crash-bang thunder starts.

Ugh - there it goes. It makes me remember that other time when there was thunder - that awful time last Easter.

Shall I tell you about it?

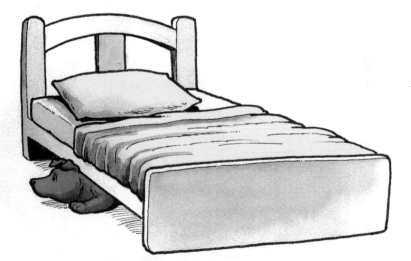

My name is Loompy - not very elegant, perhaps, but I'm afraid I'm not either: just a smallish, brownish and - er - fattish sort of dog.

I've lived with Uncle Joachim and Auntie Annemarie for as long as I can remember - and the children: lots of German children.

I left my mummy and daddy when I was just a puppy to come and live here: and all the children have left their mummies and daddies so that they can come to school in our city, Singapore. Their parents are missionaries. They leave Germany and go to other countries, telling people about Jesus. In those other countries, people wear different sorts of clothes, and eat different sorts of food. I can't imagine never having good German sausage, or cheese, or cake, but it seems some people do live without them. But it's not only food and clothes - it's the words they use. They're all different too, so the children can't go to school there because they wouldn't understand anything.

That's where Uncle Joachim and Auntie Annemarie and I come in ... we make up the family for all the German children here. We look after them while they go to the German school here in Singapore, and then they see their mummies and daddies in the holidays. I haven't seen my mummy and daddy since I came here: but I don't mind. I play with Rachel and all the others.

It was Rachel who told me all that - about why they were all here.

I remember when Rachel was just a tiny puppy - baby, I mean. Rachel belongs to Uncle Joachim. He used to put her bed outside on the grass, and I'd guard it.

I guarded it very well - all the time when I wasn't chasing Thomas and Matthias around on their bikes. That was great fun. They could go faster than I could, but I could bark louder!

The girls had a sort of kennel in the garden, too: they called it a playhouse. Sometimes they'd call, "Loompy! Come in and play!" And I'd go in and be part of the family, sitting, and begging, and having biscuits: you know the sort of thing.

6

The boys had a playhouse too - but it was up a tree in the jungly part of the garden. Have you ever heard anything so silly? I don't think I was built for climbing trees, so I just lay at the bottom, and watched, and guarded.

When it got too hot, I'd wander in and flop down on the nice cool tiled floors in the big house and take a nap. Actually, that's where you'd most often find me during the day when the children were at school.

Those were the only times I was sad - when all the bigger children went off in the minibus to school and left me behind. Thomas, Matthias and the rest would all wave out of the window. I tried to wag my tail in return, but it went slower and slower as the minibus pulled away and stopped completely when the minibus disappeared round the corner.

Sometimes they'd even all go out - Uncle Joachim and Auntie Annemarie too. I was hardly ever allowed to go, I can't think why. I'm sure there was still some space on the floor - a Loompy-shaped space. I tried - I really tried. I'd chase them, just in case they'd forgotten me by mistake... but no. Uncle Joachim would stop the minibus, take me back, and close the gates behind me. That made me really sad, being left on my own. It was terrible.

The only thing that was worse than that was thunder.

Oh yes - that's what I was going to tell you about.

CHAPTER 2

The Big Thunderstorm

It was Easter Sunday.   Everyone is very excited and happy in our big house at Easter: Rachel says it's because Jesus came back to life again after He'd died. All I really understand is that they have special things to eat, and if I'm in the right place at the right time and beg especially well, I get some too ...

So it was a very happy day. Until after dinner.

Then just as the big clock in the hall was striking three, Uncle Joachim said, "Right - everyone ready?"

I wagged my tail. I was ready. I was always ready. For anything.

Everyone trooped out of the front door, laughing and chattering - and started to climb into the minibus.

"Look, poor Loompy - his tail's drooping already!" Thomas leaned out of the window.

"We'll be back soon, Loompy, I promise!" That was Rachel.

Auntie Annemarie gave me a farewell pat. "Good girl - stay now, look after the house for us!"

I turned and walked slowly back to the house and round onto the veranda where I usually slept. I didn't have the energy to chase the minibus today.

Special day, indeed! It might be special for them, but it didn't feel very special for me.

I jumped heavily onto the comfortable old cushion, turned round a few times and settled down to wait. I wasn't really sulking, just resigned.

I was keeping one eye open, as usual, so I did

vaguely notice that it had got rather dark. But it still
took me totally by surprise -

CRASH!

Help, no, it mustn't get me, quick, quick, under
Auntie Annemarie's desk, safe there, hurry now, round
the corner, don't skid, faster - oh no, there it goes
again, soggy paws, never mind, *hurry* - oh NO!

The front door was shut.

Howl! What was I to do now? CRASH! It's getting
closer, whatever you do, RUN! Faster, don't let it
catch me, blow all the puddles, soggy tummy too,
down the drive, quick as you can, good job the gates are
open, don't look round - CRASH! and that horrid
sudden light ... head down, keep going, oh dear, getting out of breath now, puff, pant .. and what's this?

Oh, one of those bits with lots of cars and buses roaring past - if I can get across here, maybe it won't be able to follow me - careful now - phew, made it ...

And on, and on, a noisy, soggy, nightmare journey, until finally the crashing thunder stopped. The rain switched off as suddenly as it started, and I sank down, exhausted, under a tree.

After a few minutes shut-eye, I opened them again and for the first time looked at my surroundings.

But what was this - the tall, towering blocks all round me, strange trees, strange drains, strange smells - and always the roar of traffic in my poor bedraggled ears?

There was no doubt about it. I didn't know where I was.

In fact, I was lost.

Chapter 3

Looking for Loompy

Of course, when they all came back - CHAOS reigned!
(Rachel told me all about it much later, her fair hair
swinging in its bunches, like spaniels' ears, as she
whispered to me.)

They very soon realized I wasn't there. For a
start, I didn't rush out to say, "Hello, welcome back,
anyone for hide and seek?" like I usually did.

"Loompy!"

"Uncle Joachim, where's Loompy?"

Thomas chased round the side of the house to the veranda. "She's not in her bed - where can she have gone?"

"I wish we'd taken her with us!"

Uncle Joachim and Auntie Annemarie looked at each other. "That storm..." said Auntie Annemarie slowly. "Loompy must have been terrified! And she couldn't get indoors. Perhaps she ran off somewhere to hide."

Uncle Joachim organized the older children to do a street-by-street search near the house. Then he jumped back into the minibus and drove slowly round the whole district, looking carefully all the time.

But when they got back to the house, all the reports were the same: no smallish, brownish, - er - fattish -

dogs to be seen. In fact, no dogs at all. For in Singapore, dogs aren't allowed out on their own, only with owners and leads.

"At least Loompy has her collar on," said Uncle Joachim. "So she's got the tag with her registra-

14

tion number on it. I'll ring the Registration Board and tell them she's missing."

Tea that night was a miserable meal, Rachel said. Where I always sat and begged for titbits, there was no one. Where I always lay under the fan, one eye open, waiting for a final game before bedtime - there was no one.

"Daddy, where will Loompy sleep tonight?" asked Rachel.

"Will she find anything to eat?" Matthias was always thinking about food.

"How will she find her way home in the dark?"

"She *will* come back - won't she, Uncle Joachim?"

"I don't know the answer to all those questions," said Uncle Joachim slowly. "I think the best thing we can do is pray for her - pray that the Lord Jesus will look

after her, wherever she is, and bring her safely home to us."

And so, as each of the children went to bed, they prayed. That's what Rachel said. They talked to Jesus. About *me* ...

And, several miles away, I curled up, exhausted, under a clump of trees at the edge of a strange food centre, with the remains of someone's chicken-and-rice for supper.

CHAPTER 4

We won't give up!

Back at the big house, the children were up way before breakfast time, eager to see if Loompy was back.

But no - no sign of Loompy.

After breakfast, they prayed again. The Lord knew everything - He knew exactly where Loompy was. And He could do anything - He could show her the way back to the big house on the quiet, leafy street...

It was still holiday time, so no one had to go to school. Uncle Joachim drove the minibus round the

streets again, and everyone peered out of the windows, looking, looking...

"Do you think ..." Auntie Annemarie said very quietly so the children couldn't hear, "If she was so frightened, do you think Loompy might have been knocked down by a car?"

"Or picked up by a police patrol, and destroyed as a stray?" Uncle Joachim muttered back.

"But she had her collar on," Auntie Annemarie pointed out. "Though I suppose someone might have stolen her to use as a watchdog."

"It's no use thinking like that!" Uncle Joachim turned the corner sharply and headed for home. "We must just keep praying."

But nights and mornings came and went, came and went: the fourth day; the fifth day; the sixth day.

"You know," said Uncle Joachim sadly to his wife, "I really don't think there's much chance of Loompy coming back now."

Night and morning, night and morning: the seventh day; the eighth day.

"You know, children," began Auntie Annemarie gently when bedtime came on the eighth day, "it's very unlikely that Loompy will come back to us now. Perhaps it would be a good idea to ask Jesus to send us another dog instead."

"*Another* dog?" Thomas looked at her in great surprise. "We don't want *another* dog - Loompy's our dog!"

"She'll come back - she will!"

"No other dog could be like Loompy."

(I like that ... No other dog could be like me ...)

"Jesus will bring her back - we asked Him to!"

"And we haven't finished praying yet."

"And we won't finish - not until Loompy comes back!"

Auntie Annemarie looked across at her husband. Uncle Joachim shrugged. Then, to the children, he said, "You must pray as Jesus shows you. I hope you won't be disappointed," he added, half to himself.

And so the children prayed on, night and morning, night and morning! The ninth day; the tenth day ...

Still talking to Jesus - about me.

CHAPTER 5

Loompy Alone

Ten days, they said it was: but I'm sure it must have been longer. It felt more like ten weeks, or ten years. Ten years without a square meal! Ten years dodging in and out of scary, screechy traffic; ten years of no Rachel ...!

And thirsty! One thing you can usually be sure of in Singapore is that it will rain pretty regularly. Like every day at around four o'clock. But it had hardly rained at all since that dreadful Easter Sunday.

So, what was a dog to do, without even a decent puddle to lap?

And hungry! Another thing you can usually be sure of in Singapore is food. There are hundreds of places for people to eat, indoors and outdoors. And the smell: mouth-watering, I tell you! But hardly a scrap left lying around for a poor dog trying to keep body and soul together ..

I realized I was fast becoming a smallish, brownish, *thinnish* sort of dog.

And my paws! Singapore, they say, is a garden city - plenty of green, plenty of trees. All I can say is, there are plenty of roads and pavements too, and most of them seemed to get in my way .. and there's nothing that makes for sore paws more than chasing across six lanes of traffic before those little lights start flashing at you.

So, you can see I wasn't feeling on top form exactly. More like bottom form.

I'd just crossed one of those six-lots-of-cars roads, and was snuffling half-heartedly around another outdoor eating centre, but without much hope - when suddenly I saw her!

A girl with fair skin, and fair hair in bunches, coming out of a nearby shop. Rachel! She was with a little Asian boy. Don't know who he was, didn't matter anyway.

With a sudden new energy, I bounded over to them, tail wagging nineteen to the dozen, "I'm so happy to see you! Oh Rachel, I'm so ..."

The children turned round as they heard me.

It wasn't Rachel.

I skidded to a halt, my tail drooping between my legs. I gave a kind of half-bark, half-whimper.

"Are you from the flats?" asked the fair-haired girl. "You'd better go home!"

I looked at her, my tail drooping even further. What did she think I was *trying* to do?

"Come on, Jack." The children went off up the road with their shopping.

Slowly, I followed.

Why not?

Perhaps, since she looked so much like Rachel, this other fair girl would be kind to me.

CHAPTER 6

Loompy - Mission Dog

A few yards up the road, the children turned into a long driveway and made their way around the back of some buildings.

I was still following.

"Mummy, here's the shopping!" called the girl. "And come and look at this dog who's followed us home - I think she likes me!"

"Thanks, Amy." Not only her mother but her father as well came out to meet me.

Not forgetting my manners, I sat down and held out a paw in greeting.

"Why, what a well-behaved dog! She's no stray," said Amy's father.

I laid back my ears, pleased, and gave a little bark of agreement.

"She must be lost," said Amy's mother. "But she's got a collar on, and a tag ... Let's see."

I sat very still as they peered at the tag. "Good - a registration number!"

Amy's father went straight to the phone. He was soon back.

"You'll never guess," he said, a huge grin spreading across his face. "The lady at the Registration Office says that this dog was reported lost ten days ago - by a Mr Joachim Wesner!"

"Uncle Joachim!" Amy looked at her father in amazement.

I pricked up my ears at once - Uncle Joachim!

"That's right - Uncle Joachim who looks after all the German children from our Mission!"

Amy's father bent down and gave me a pat. "But it's extraordinary - their big house is right across the city from our Headquarters building here: it's miles and miles away!"

"I remember we went there for tea," said Amy. "Lots of lovely German cake!" She looked down at me wonderingly. "Do you think she could have known

we were all part of the same big Mission family?"

"I'm sure I don't know," said Amy's mother, smiling; "but I think Jesus must have been looking after her!"

I'd hardly finished the biscuits and the big bowl of lovely cool water that Amy gave me, when I heard a familiar sound - the best sound in the world!

As the minibus came up the long drive, I dashed out of the door, sore paws forgotten, and hurtled up to it. I couldn't wait for Auntie Annemarie to stop and get out, but threw myself against the door and window, barking my best "Welcome-oh-I-*am*-glad-to-see-you!" ever.

"Steady!" Auntie Annemarie finally managed to get the door open, and out they all tumbled, she and Uncle Joachim, Thomas .. and Rachel. There was a bit of a confused heap for the next few minutes, with lots of hugs, licks and laughter.

"Two and a half million people in Singapore," Uncle Joachim was saying to Amy's father, "and Loompy chose to follow your Amy. Isn't that wonderful?"

Intelligent, I call it. Discerning.

"Jesus showed her," said Rachel, her arm still round me. "Like we asked Him to."

Uncle Joachim looked at her. "Yes, that's true," he said. "We would have given up - but you children didn't."

I pushed my nose into Rachel's hand and licked it.

"Loompy's a real Mission dog," said Amy's mother. "I wonder if she knows it?"

"Loompy, missing dog. Loompy, Mission dog!" chanted Thomas, bouncing round me until I felt dizzy.

I think it's safe to come out from under this bed now. Loompy, Mission dog. I like that.

Note to parents

The Overseas Missionary Fellowship provides schooling for the children of its missionaries. This includes English-language schools in Japan and Malaysia, and homes for children attending an intermission school in the Philippines. German-speaking children attend the German and Swiss schools in Singapore and live in homes such as the one featured in this book.

While every effort is made to provide missionaries' children with the best possible home and educational situations, this is not always easy. Why not take a moment to pray with your child for missionary children who may have to be away from their parents.